Tables
Easy Word Essentials
Volume 4

M.L. HUMPHREY

TITLES BY M.L. HUMPHREY

CONTENTS

INTRODUCTION

In *Word for Beginners* I covered the basics of working in Word and in *Intermediate Word* I covered more intermediate-level topics. But I realized that some users will just want to know about a specific topic and not buy a guide that covers a variety of other topics that aren't of interest to them.

So this series of guides is meant to address that need. Each guide in the series covers one specific topic such as formatting, tables, or track changes.

I'm going to assume in these guides that you have a basic understanding of how to navigate Word, although each guide does include an Appendix with a brief discussion of basic terminology to make sure that we're on the same page.

The guides are written using Word 2013, which should be similar enough for most users of Word to follow, but anyone using a version of Word prior to Word 2007 probably won't be able to use them effectively.

Also, keep in mind that the content in these guides is drawn from *Word for Beginners* and *Intermediate Word*, so if you think you'll end up buying all of these guides you're probably better off just buying *Word for Beginners* and *Intermediate Word* instead.

Having said all of that, let's talk tables.

TABLES:
INSERTING

A table is essentially a grid of spaces. It can have a range of spaces across a row (one, two, three, four, five, etc.) and any number of rows you want. Tables are useful for providing a structure to information that you want to provide your reader. I find tables are the most granular way to control exactly where text appears on the page. (Which isn't to say that I don't use numbered or bulleted lists. I use them all the time. But when I really need precision in terms of how items are spaced, etc. I will sometimes turn to tables.)

So. Let's talk about how to insert a basic table into your document.

First, go to the Insert tab. Next, find the Tables section on the left-hand side and click on the dropdown arrow under Table. Use your mouse to select the number of columns and rows you want in your table by hovering your mouse over the first square on the top left and then moving it to the right and down until you've selected the desired number of columns and rows. Once you have that desired number of rows and columns selected, click on the last cell and Word will insert a table into your document that has the number of columns and rows you selected.

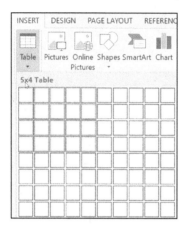

If you'd prefer, you can also insert a table into a document by going to the Tables section of the Insert tab, clicking on the arrow under Table, and choosing Insert Table from the dropdown menu. This brings up the Insert Table dialogue box where you can specify the exact number of columns and rows you want.

In newer versions of Word you also have the option to insert an Excel spreadsheet or use one of a handful of

Quick Tables. Personally, I don't use either of those options. When I want to insert a table I want to format it to my tastes and the Quick Tables options aren't even close to what I would choose. And embedding an Excel file in your Word file can be more tricky than it's worth. (I've done so in PowerPoint before and it can get a little messy.) But they are two more options if you want to try them.

And don't worry if you insert a table and then decide you need it to have more rows or more columns or the columns aren't the width you want them to be. In the next section we'll talk about how to take that basic table you inserted and format it to be exactly what you want.

TABLES:
STRUCTURE

Once you've inserted a table into your document, chances are you'll want to format it. There are many, many options for formatting a table, so let's walk through them.

COLUMN WIDTH

When you insert a table chances are the columns will have the same width and you'll want to adjust that. You have a number of options for doing so.

First, you can place your cursor over the line between two columns. Your cursor should turn into something that looks like two parallel lines with arrows pointing to the left and the right. (You'll probably only be able to see the arrows since the parallel lines will be lined up with the line separating the two columns.) Once your cursor looks like this, you can left-click on the line between the two columns and drag the line to the left or the right to change the width of the column. This will change the width of two columns at once since the other column divider lines will stay stationary.

Second, you can right click into a cell in the column you want to change and choose Table Properties from the dropdown menu. This will bring up the Table Properties dialogue box. From there go to the Column tab and change your column by entering an exact width for that column. (You can do this for all columns at once by selecting the whole table or an entire row in the table and then adjusting the value for column width. This does mean, of course, that they'll all have the same column width.)

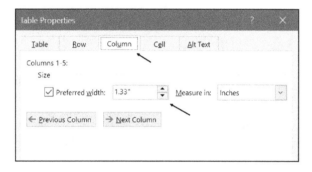

Third, you can go to the Table Tools Layout tab which should be an option once you click on some part of the table. In the Cell Size section, you can change the value for the column you're in by changing the Width value. (You can change all columns at once by selecting the whole table and changing the value, but if you only select one row and use this option it will only change the column widths for that selected row, not the entire table.)

Fourth, if you have text that you've entered into a cell, you can have Word AutoFit the width of the cell to the text you've entered by going to the Table Tools Layout tab and clicking on the dropdown arrow under AutoFit in the Cell Size section. From there choose AutoFit Contents. (Be careful if you do this and only have text in one cell, because all of your other columns will also be adjusted, but to the smallest possible width.)

ROW HEIGHT

Your options for adjusting the height of a row in your table are mostly the same as for changing the column width, although there will be some row heights you can't achieve because Word forces a minimum row height based upon font size.

First, you can place your cursor over the line dividing any rows in the table and left-click and drag to your desired height.

Second, you can right-click on any cell in a row and choose Table Properties to bring up the Table Properties dialogue box. From there go to the Row tab and input your desired row height.

Or third, you can use the Table Tools Layout tab to specify the row height by changing the number for Height in the Cell Size section.

(AutoFit is not an option for row height. It only works on column width.)

Whichever method you use, be sure to look at the table after you're done, because if you tried to specify a row height that was smaller than Word allowed, it won't change even though the number looks like it has. (To get around this, at least to a certain extent if there isn't text in that row, you can manually change the font size for the cells in that row to 1 point.)

TABLE WIDTH

An attribute of tables that I often change is the overall width of the table. To do this, right-click on the table and select Table Properties. When the Table Properties dialogue box comes up, go to the Table tab and click on the box for Preferred Width under Size and then specify the width you want for the table.

You can also go to the right-hand side of the table, hover your mouse over that outside column line until you see the two parallel lines with arrows on either side, and then left-click and drag until you have the table width you want. Just know that you may run into issues with this approach if you're trying to make a table smaller, because you can only drag so far before Word stops you because you've reached the minimum width for the last column in the table. (You can then change that column's width and keep going, but it turns out to be a multi-step process most of the time. It's still the way I usually do it, though.)

Another option if you want the table to be the width of the page is to use AutoFit. Click on the table, go to the Cell Size section of the Table Tools Layout tab, click on the dropdown arrow under AutoFit, and choose AutoFit Window.

MOVING A TABLE

If you have a table that isn't the entire width of the page, chances are you'll need to move it to where you want it on that line. To do this, place your cursor over the table. You should now see a square box appear off the side of the top left corner of the table. It will have arrows pointing in all four cardinal directions. Left-click on that box and drag the table to where you want it. (This also works for dragging the table to another location in the document.)

If you want to move the table to a different document or a significantly different location in your current document, you can also right-click on the box in the top-left corner, choose Copy or Cut from the dropdown menu, go to the new location, and Paste.

DELETING THE CONTENTS
OF A TABLE

To delete the contents of a table, you can select all of the cells in the table and then use the Delete key. The table will remain, but all of the text will be removed.

DELETING A CELL, ROW, COLUMN, OR ENTIRE TABLE

To delete an entire table, you can select all of the cells in the table and use the Backspace key. This will delete both the contents within the table as well as the table itself.

To delete a table, you can also right-click on the box in the top left corner of the table and choose Delete Table from the dropdown menu.

To delete a row, select the row you want to delete and then use the Backspace key. This will show you the Delete Cells dialogue box. Choose to Delete Entire Row and click OK.

To delete a column, select the column you want to delete and use the Backspace key. It should delete automatically.

To delete a cell, row, or column, you can right-click in a cell in the table and choose Delete Cells from the dropdown menu. This will bring up the Delete Cells dialogue box (above). From there you can choose to delete the individual cell or the entire row or column. If you delete just a cell, other cells in that row or column will have to shift to fill the space, so be careful because deleting that one cell may rearrange your information in ways you don't like.

To delete cells, columns, rows, or tables, you can also go to the Table Tools Layout tab and click on the Delete option in the Rows and Columns section. In the dropdown you can then choose to delete a cell, row, column, or the entire table.

INSERTING A CELL, ROW, OR COLUMN

If you need to add a cell, row, or column to your table there are a number of ways to do so.

To insert a cell, click into an existing cell in the table that is where you want to insert the cell. Right-click and on the dropdown menu hold your mouse over the Insert option and then choose Insert Cells from the new dropdown menu that should appear. You'll then see the Insert Cells dialogue box. You can either choose to shift cells to the right or down to make room for the new cell.

To insert a row or column, you can also click into an existing cell in the table that is where you want the new row or column, right-click, hover your mouse over the Insert option and then choose one of the insert row or column choices on the second dropdown menu.

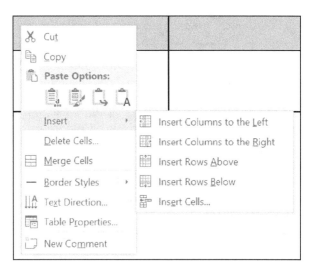

A quick way to insert a new row at the bottom of an existing table is to go to the last cell in the table (the one in the bottom right-hand corner) and then use the Tab key.

Another way to insert a new row or column is by using the Table Tools Layout tab and going to the Rows & Columns section. Click into the spot in your table where you want to insert the new row or column and then choose Insert Above or Insert Below for a row or Insert Left or Insert Right for a column.

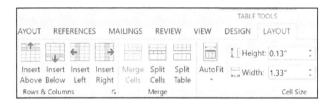

To insert multiple rows or columns at once, select multiple rows or columns in your table and then choose one of the insert options. If you select three rows and choose to insert more rows, it will insert three more rows. If you select two columns and choose to insert columns, it will insert two more columns.

SPLITTING OR MERGING CELLS

One of the nice features when working with tables in Word is that you can split cells. This means that different rows in your table can have a different number of columns in them. So if you want to put a row of labels at the top of your table where each label covers multiple columns, you can do that.

Like this:

Book Information		
Title	Pub Date	Pages

See how in this table I've created a first row that is just one cell that says Book Information, and then on the next row I have three separate columns of book information: Title, Pub Date, and Pages?

If you already have an existing table with the number of columns you need, you can insert a new row at the top and merge cells to create the header in that first row.

One way to merge the cells is to select all of the cells in the first row and then go to the Table Tools Layout tab and choose Merge Cells from the Merge section. (The Merge Cells option only shows as available when you have more than one cell selected.)

The other option is to select all of the cells in the row, right-click, and choose Merge Cells from the dropdown menu.

(Unlike in Excel, if you merge two cells with text in them, Word will keep the text from both cells in the new merged cell.)

What if instead you've built a table like this but now want to add a new column? You can't just insert a column because you have that header row with the merged cells. In that case, you can split cells in one of your existing columns to form a new column.

Using the table pictured above, I could select the cell that says Title as well as all of the cells in the column below it. (Note I'm not selecting any cell from the first row of the table.) I would then go to the Table Tools Layout tab and choose Split Cells from the Merge section. This brings up the Split Cells dialogue box that allows me to tell Word how many rows and columns to split the cells into.

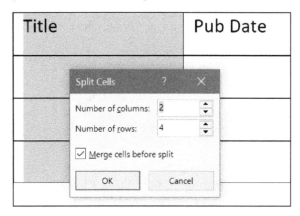

In this case, because I want two columns out of the one that I have now, I say two columns and four rows.

If you already have text in more than just the first cell you've chosen to split, uncheck the box that says "Merge cells before split." Also, if you do have text in the cells you're splitting check after you split the cells that your text in the cells is where you think it should be.

You can also split an individual cell by right-clicking and choosing Split Cells, but that only works on one cell at a time.

SPLIT TABLE

You can take an existing table and split it into two tables. Usually this won't be necessary because, as we'll discuss in a moment, with large tables you can format them so the top row(s) repeat on each page. But I do use this sometimes when formatting the table of contents in my print books. It gives me the most control over how a table of contents that continues onto a second page appears.

To take an existing table and split it, select the row that you want to be the first row in the second table. Next, click on Split Table in the Merge section of the Table Tools Layout tab. Instead of one table with continuous rows, you'll now see two tables that were split apart at the row you selected. In the image below, I had selected row 3 before using Split Table.

1		
2		
3		

4		
5		

(I should also note that Split Table did not want to work for me when I was using a table that had a different number of columns in each row, so if you think you're going to split a table, try to do so before you split your columns.)

SPACING BETWEEN CELLS

You can also format a table so that there are spaces between each of the cells in the table. Like this:

See how there's space between all of the cells in this table instead of just a line?

To do this, click on your table, go to the Alignment section of the Table Tools Layout tab, and click on Cell Margins. This will bring up the Table Options dialogue box.

If you click on Allow Spacing Between Cells you can specify a space that's wide enough to be visible like I did here.

You can also do this by right-clicking on your table, choosing Table Properties from the dropdown menu, and then clicking on Options on the Table tab.

TABLES:
FORMATTING

Alright. We've talked about how to build your table. Now it's time to talk about all the formatting that you can do within the cells of the table. This is probably where I spend most of my time when I'm working on tables.

TABLE STYLES

If you don't want to mess with specific formatting for your table, but do want it to look like more than a set of generic boxes, the simplest way to do that is to apply a Table Style to your table. Table Styles can be found in the Table Tools Design tab in the Table Styles section. The first few entries are just basic black and white options with some lines made invisible or with some gray shading to separate lines. If you click on the arrow with a line in the bottom right corner, though, you can expand the list of options to see a number of additional options, some of which use colors.

To apply a table style, click on your table and then click on the style you want. This will overwrite any line or background fill or font color you already applied to the table. (Which is what we're about to discuss.)

To the left of the available styles are six checkboxes. Check these based upon whether you have a header row, total row, or want special formatting on your first column or last column. Depending on the style, that will mean different things for those rows and columns, usually bolding or color differences, but also sometimes differences in the border lines.

FONT, FONT SIZE, FONT COLOR, ETC.

If you want to change the font, font size, text color, add bold or italics to text in a cell, or any other basic text formatting, you do so in the same way that you would format text in other parts of your document.

For the entire table, click on the box in the top left corner to select all cells in the table first. If it's for specific cells, select those cells. If it's for specific text, select the word(s) you want to format. Next, go to the Font section of the Home tab and make your formatting selections.

Be careful with changing the font or font size, because the table will automatically resize itself to accommodate your text to make sure it remains visible.

BACKGROUND FILL (SHADING)

I use the first row of most tables as a header row that contains labels for each column. To distinguish this row from the rows that have the content, I often will color the cells in the row. Like this:

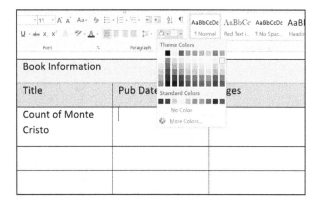

The first two rows have shading to designate them as header rows and then the actual data the table is providing starts on row three.

To add shading to cells, select the cells where you want to add shading, go to the Paragraph section of the Home tab, and click on the arrow next to the paint bucket on the bottom right-hand side (that says Shading if you hold your mouse over it) and choose a color from the dropdown menu.

There are seventy colors you can choose from in Word 2013. If that's not enough (for example, you need to use a corporate color), you can click on More Colors at the bottom. This will bring up the Colors dialogue box. From there you can either choose a color from the honeycomb of colors on the Standard tab or you can go to the Custom tab and enter the RGB values for the color you need. (My last client had a corporate color palette and when they published the corporate colors guideline it include the RGB values for each of the corporate colors, making them easy to incorporate into a document.)

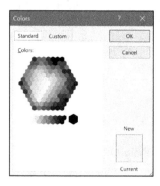 

If you don't want to use the Home tab options, you can also click on Shading from the Table Styles section of the Table Tools Design tab.

Or you can open the Borders and Shading dialogue box from the Paragraph section of the Home tab by clicking on the Borders dropdown and choosing Borders and Shading and then going to the Shading tab.

TABLE LINE STYLES, WEIGHT, AND COLOR

Another aspect of a table that you might want to adjust is the appearance of the lines that form the table. For example, in the table of contents for my print books I use a table, but I don't want those lines visible, so for those tables I change the line style to No Border. I've also had situations where I wanted a thicker outer border around a table and then thinner lines within the table.

To change the lines on a table that you've already created, first go to the Borders section of the Table Tools Design tab and choose the line style, weight (thickness), and color you want.

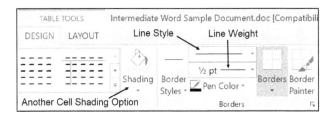

Next, select the cells where you want to apply that line style, weight, and color. (If it's all, just select the whole table.) Now, go back to the Borders section of the Table Tools Design tab and click what border lines you want to place around those cells. (If it's all borders then it's the All Borders option. If it's just the outside edge of the table, then it's the Outside Borders option.)

You can use more than one style/weight/color on the lines in your table, but if you do so be careful about the order in which you format your cells. For example, if I wanted a thicker outside border, I would apply the inside border formatting to all cells first and then do the outside border second. Because if I did the outside border first and then tried to format the inside borders differently, it would take me more steps since I couldn't just use the All Border option to format the cells along the edge of the table.

You can also apply more than one type of border to a specific cell. So you can choose top border and bottom border for the same cell, for example.

And don't forget that you need to set your line formatting first and then choose the cells and type of border to apply. If you don't do that you'll be applying the existing line formatting to your cells. (Don't worry if you do get it out of order. It'll be pretty obvious and then you just fix it. I've done it a number of times myself.)

If it sounds a little too complicated to you to figure out how to get that line on the bottom of the second cell from the right to be formatted in a specific way using the Border dropdown menu, then try the Border Painter instead. As above, you need to set the way you want the line to look in terms of weight, color, and style before you use the Border Painter. Once you've done that, go to the Borders section of the Table Tools Design tab and click on the Border Painter option.

Your cursor should turn into a little paintbrush. Next, click on the lines in your table that you want to format that way and Word will apply the format to just that specific line in that cell. (Which means it's a much slower option than using the Borders dropdown if you're trying to format a number of cells.)

You can also choose from a set of pre-defined line styles that are available either in the Borders section of the Table Tools Design tab under Border Styles, or by right-clicking on your table and choosing Border Styles from the dropdown menu. Both options will bring up a set of line colors/weights/styles that you can choose from and then the Border Painter tool that will allow you to apply the style to your table.

And, finally, another option for formatting the borders in your table is to go to the Paragraph section of the Home tab, click on the Borders dropdown menu in the bottom right corner and either choose your line types if that's all you need or go to Borders and Shading to bring up the Borders and Shading dialogue box that will allow you to specify line color, weight, and type as well.

USING THE BORDER SAMPLER

If you have a line in a table that is formatted exactly the way you want already, you can sample it to copy its formatting. To do this, go to the Borders section of the Table Tools Design tab and click on the arrow under Border Styles. Then click on the Border Sampler option at the bottom of the dropdown. Your cursor will turn into a little eye dropper. Next, go to the line with the formatting you want and click on it. Word will take the formatting from that sample line and change the line style, weight, and color to match it. You can then apply that line style to the rest of your table or to other tables in your document.

(You can also access the Border Sampler by right-clicking on your table and choosing the Border Styles option and then choosing Border Sampler from there.)

CHANGE TEXT DIRECTION

By default, the text in the cells in a table will be aligned from left to right as if you were reading a line of text. If you would like it to instead be perpendicular to the normal direction of text, you can change this by going to the Table Tools Layout tab and clicking on Text Direction in the Alignment section on the right-hand side. There are only three options, and each click will change the direction of the text until you cycle back to normal.

ALIGN TEXT WITHIN A CELL

You can align text within a cell in a total of nine configurations. You can choose to place text either at the Top, Center, or Bottom of a cell and also to the Left, Center, or Right of the cell. To choose the combination you want, select the cells, go to the Alignment section of the Table Tools Layout tab and click on the image of the alignment you prefer. (If you only have one line of text in a cell, some of the alignment choices will appear to be identical.)

REPEAT A ROW AT THE TOP
OF EACH PAGE

If you have a particularly long table that stretches across multiple pages, you should repeat the header row at the top of each page. Don't do this manually. One little edit and your whole document will be messed up. (Or one change to that header row and you'll have to make it on every single page. Ugh.)

To tell Word to repeat a row at the top of each page, click into one cell of the row, go to the Data section of the Table Tools Layout tab, and click on Repeat Header Rows. If you have more than one row you want to repeat, you can select cells in multiple rows and follow the steps above. The rows that repeat need to be the first ones in your table. You can't have the third row be the one that repeats. (Word won't let you click on the option unless it's the first row or row(s).)

Another way to specify that a row needs to repeat on each page is to click into a cell in the row you want to repeat, right-click, choose Table Properties, go to the Row tab, and click on Repeat As Header Row At The Top Of Each Page. You can do this for multiple rows at once, by selecting one cell from each row before you right-click.

TABLES:
OTHER

If you have tables that include a lot of data in them and you haven't completed your analysis, I'd recommend using Microsoft Excel for the analysis portion. For me, tables in Word are just to display information, they're not where you sort your information or analyze it. However, Word does allow for some manipulation of your data. So I'm going to cover it here, but it's not what I recommend doing. Excel is far better for this sort of thing than Word. And as long as you've built your table with the right number of rows and columns it's easy to copy and paste data from Excel into Word.

Anyway.

SORTING

You can actually sort lines of text in Word without having them in a table. You could have a list of five words in Word, each on a separate line, and have Word sort them by using the A to Z option in the Paragraph section of the Home tab. (Why you would ever do so, I don't know. But it is possible.)

It's far more likely, though, that you'd want to Sort entries in a table. For example, in the table above where I was listing information on books, maybe I'd realize after I'd created the table that I wanted to sort them by number of pages. Or by author name. Or by book title.

All are possible in Word.

To sort the entries in a table, select the whole table, go to the Table Tools Layout tab and click on the A to Z Sort option in the Data section on the right-hand side. It will bring up the Sort dialogue box.

If you have a header row in your table, tell Word and it will label your options using the labels in your header row. Otherwise it will just number the columns.

You can then choose to sort your table by the values in up to three different columns.

For each column you can choose to sort in either ascending or descending order and you can specify to Word whether the contents of the cells should be treated as text, numbers, or dates. The first column you list will be the main one used in the sort. The second listed column will only be used if two rows have the same value for the first column.

Your sort options here are not as sophisticated as those available in Excel, but for a basic sort, they're not bad.

FORMULAS

Again, I'd encourage you to use Excel for something like this. But if you don't want to listen to me, Word does have a formula option in the Table Tools Layout tab.

To use this option, click into a cell in your table and then go to the Table Tools Layout tab and click on Formula. This will bring up a Formula dialogue box. Word may suggest a formula to you based on the contents of the table, but it may not. If it doesn't, you can go down to the Paste function option at the bottom of the dialogue box and choose from the list of functions in the dropdown menu. That will paste an empty version of that function into the Formula line. You'll need to know what the function does (because there's nothing to explain it to you) and also be able to complete it yourself.

Here are a few options you can use:

=SUM(LEFT) will sum all numbers in columns to the left of the cell you're in

=AVERAGE(LEFT) will average the numeric values in the columns to the left of the cell you're in

=PRODUCT(LEFT) will multiply the numeric values in the columns to the left of the cell you're in

=COUNT(LEFT) will count the number of cells to the left of the one you're in that have numeric values

* * *

Note that for the formulas, Word only looks at numeric values. It won't count, for example, cells with text in them. You can change any of the above formulas to use RIGHT, ABOVE, and BELOW instead to apply the formulas to cells to the right in a row or above or below in a column.

To specify the format of your result, use the Number format dropdown choices in the dialogue box. Unfortunately, those number formats are only available for when you use a formula. So if you have a few columns with numbers you want to add in the final column, you can only format the final column where you add those values together. (Another reason to do most of this in Excel where you could format all of the columns the same.)

CONCLUSION

So that's the basics of tables in Word.
 If you get stuck, reach out at:

mlhumphreywriter@gmail.com

I'm happy to help. I don't check that email account every single day but I do check it regularly and will try to find you the answer if I don't know it.
 Good luck with it!

APPENDIX A: BASIC TERMINOLOGY

TAB

I refer to the menu choices at the top of the screen (File, Home, Insert, Design, Page Layout, References, Mailings, Review, View, Developer) as tabs. If you click on one you'll see that the way it's highlighted sort of looks like an old-time filing system.

CLICK

If I tell you to click on something, that means to use your mouse (or trackpad) to move the arrow on the screen over to a specific location and left-click or right-click on the option. (See the next definition for the difference between left-click and right-click).

If you left-click, this selects the item. If you right-click, this generally creates a dropdown list of options to choose from. If I don't tell you which to do, left- or right-click, then left-click.

LEFT-CLICK/RIGHT-CLICK

If you look at your mouse or your trackpad, you generally have two flat buttons to press. One is on the left side, one is on the right. If I say left-click that means to press down on the button on the left. If I say right-click that means press down on the button on the right.

Now, as I sadly learned when I had to upgrade computers and ended up with an HP Envy, not all track pads have the left- and right-hand buttons. In that case, you'll basically want to press on either the bottom left-hand side of the track pad or the bottom right-hand side of the trackpad. Since you're working blind it may take a little trial and error to get the option you want working. (Or is that just me?)

SELECT OR HIGHLIGHT

If I tell you to select text, that means to left-click at the end of the text you want to select, hold that left-click, and move your cursor to the other end of the text you want to select.

Another option is to use the Shift key. Go to one end of the text you want to select. Hold down the shift key and use the arrow keys to move to the other end of the text you want to select. If you arrow up or down, that will select an entire row at a time.

With both methods, which side of the text you start on doesn't matter. You can start at the end and go to the beginning or start at the beginning and go to the end. Just start at one end or the other of the text you want to select.

The text you've selected will then be highlighted in gray.

If you need to select text that isn't touching you can do this by selecting your first section of text and then holding down the Ctrl key and selecting your second section of text using your mouse. (You can't arrow to the second section of text or you'll lose your already selected text.)

DROPDOWN MENU

If you right-click in a Word document, you will see what I'm going to refer to as a dropdown menu. (Sometimes it will actually drop upward if you're towards the bottom of the document.)

A dropdown menu provides you a list of choices to select from.

There are also dropdown menus available for some of the options listed under the tabs at the top of the screen. For example, if you go to the Home tab, you'll see small arrows below or next to some of the options, like the numbered list option in the paragraph section. If you click on those arrows, you'll see that there are multiple choices you can choose from listed on a dropdown menu.

DIALOGUE BOX

Dialogue boxes are pop-up boxes that cover specialized settings. As just mentioned, if you click on an expansion arrow, it will often open a dialogue box that contains more choices than are visible in that section. When you right-click in a Word document and choose Font, Paragraph, or Hyperlink that also opens dialogue boxes.

Dialogue boxes allow the most granular level of control over an option. For example, the Paragraph Dialogue Box has more options available than in the Paragraph section of the Home tab.

(This may not apply to you, but be aware that if you have more than one Word document open and open a dialogue box in one of those documents, you may not be able to move to the other documents you have open until you close the dialogue box.)

CONTROL SHORTCUTS

I'll occasionally mention control shortcuts that you can use to perform tasks. When I reference them I'll do so by writing it as Ctrl + a capital letter. To use the shortcut just hold down the control key while typing the letter specified. Even though the letter will be capitalized, you don't need to use the capitalized version for the shortcut to work. For example, holding down the Ctrl key and the s key at the same time will save your document. I'll write this as Ctrl + S.

ABOUT THE AUTHOR

M.L. Humphrey is a former stockbroker with a degree in Economics from Stanford and an MBA from Wharton who has spent close to twenty years as a regulator and consultant in the financial services industry.

You can reach M.L. at mlhumphreywriter@gmail.com or at mlhumphrey.com.

Tables are an incredibly useful tool to use in Microsoft Word. They allow you to easily organize and display data and information.

This guide covers how to use them, including formatting them and sorting data stored in them.

ISBN 978-1-950902-28-6
50799

9 781950 902286